The Divinized Person

Dennis J. Billy, C.Ss.R.

En Route Books and Media, LLC
Saint Louis, MO

⊕ *ENROUTE*
Make the time

En Route Books and Media, LLC
5705 Rhodes Avenue
St. Louis, MO 63109

Contact us at **contact@enroutebooksandmedia.com**

Cover Credit: Sebastian Mahfood

Copyright 2023 Dennis J. Billy, C.Ss.R.

ISBN-13: 979-8-88870-105-8
Library of Congress Control Number: 2023950849

All rights reserved. No part of this book may be reproduced, stored in a retrieval system, or transmitted in any form, or by any means, electronic, mechanical, photocopying, or otherwise, without the prior written permission of the author.

For Michelle and Jeffrey

God became man,
so man might become divine.

St. Athanasius

Table of Contents

Introduction 1

Chapter 1: Jesus Christ: Icon of the Father 5
Chapter 2: The Human Person: Icon of Christ 25
Chapter 3: Contemplating the Human Person 45
Chapter 4: Befriending the Human Person 65
Chapter 5: Becoming a Divinized Person 87

Conclusion 107

Introduction

Scripture tells us that man was created in the image and likeness of God (Gn 1:26). This book explores the meaning of this statement. It uses the image of an icon as a way of understanding what it means to be a person whose very being reflects the mystery of the divine. Icons are instruments of prayer, works of art that combine image and symbol in a way that opens a window to eternity for the person beholding them. Unlike the three-dimensional depictions of Western art, icons come from Eastern Christianity and juxtapose images and symbols to convey a sense of the beyond. The two-dimensional character of an icon is intended to lead the person beholding it into another dimension, that of the world beyond time and space. We can pray before the icon vocally by talking to the person or persons represented there. Or we can meditate on the story being told through the images and symbols. Or we can simply gaze upon the icon in silence. Icons are sacramentals. They are visible representations intended to lead us to an encounter with the divine.

The book consists of five chapters. Chapter one, "Jesus Christ: Icon of the Father," presents Jesus, the Word-made-flesh, as an expression par excellence of what it means to be a window into the mystery of the divine. It views Jesus as one who mediates the presence of God to all who behold him. Chapter two, "The Human Person: Icon of Christ," presents each human being as an image of Christ, the perfect man. Although that image may be tarnished by sin, the dignity of the person never disappears and can be restored by prayer and the grace of the Holy Spirit. Chapter three, "Contemplating the Human Person," looks at every dimension of our human makeup and offers some interpretive lenses for discovering how each person can lead us to an encounter with God. It presents a person as a living icon meant to be pondered and prayed with and looked upon as a window that mediates the mystery of the divine. Chapter four, "Befriending the Human Person," examines the relationship between freedom and holiness and emphasizes the importance of encountering others on every level of their human makeup. When we do so, we discover how each person can help us be aware of unseen truths about Christ and his mystical body of believers. Chapter five, "Becoming a Divinized Person," looks at how the grace of the Spirit divinizes us as individuals and incorporates us as collective members of Jesus, the New Adam's glorified body. It preserves both the individual and corporate dimensions of our relations with Christ and one another. Each chapter ends with a series of relevant reflection questions and a prayer to the Holy Spirit for help in our journey to God.

Each of us is a living, flesh-and-blood icon of Christ. The goal of the Christian life is to cooperate with the grace of the Spirit so that Christ's life might shine through us to such an extent that we can proclaim with the Apostle Paul with our words and actions that "…it is no longer I who live, but it is Christ who lives in me" (Gal 2:20). For most of us, it will take a lifetime (and beyond) for us to reach such a point of holiness. Be that as it may, the key question each of us must face is whether the gap between where we are and where God wants us to be is getting larger or smaller. The purpose of this book is to help us see more clearly God's vision for us so that we will time and again always be ready to choose the latter.

Chapter One

Jesus Christ: Icon of the Father

According to the orthodox Christian faith, Jesus Christ is true God and true man, fully human and fully divine. In his divinity, he is the *Logos*, the Word of God, the Only Begotten Son of the Father. In his humanity, he is created and like us in all things but sin. In his divinity, he is the Second Person of the Most Holy Trinity. In his humanity, he reveals to us what it means to be fully human, fully redeemed, fully ourselves, unburdened by the ravages of sin and death. In his divinity, he is God himself, existing before all else that is. In his humanity, he is an icon of God, a window into eternity, a passageway to heaven.

In this chapter, we will see how, created in God's image and likeness, we, too, are icons of God (however tarnished by sin we may be). Through the grace of the Spirit that was unleashed on the world by virtue of Jesus' passion and death, resurrection, and ascension to heaven, we have the capacity to become "friends of God" (how the saints were called in the early Church) and to lead others into such friendship.[1]

Instruments of Prayer

Icons come from the Eastern Christian tradition, both Catholic and Orthodox, and are meant to be instruments of prayer, windows to eternity, that lead those of us who pray before them out of measured time (*Chronos*) into sacred time (*Kairos*). In Eastern liturgies, they mark off the sanctuary from the praying faithful, not to separate them from the divine but as a means of drawing them from earthly to heavenly realities. They are unlike the typical three-dimensional paintings common to Western art, especially since the Renaissance, but represent a juxtaposition of image and symbol, story, and sign, in a combination that creates an unexpected two-dimensional visual tension, specifically designed to lead others to a contemplation of the beyond. When we gaze upon an

---

[1] See Peter Brown, *The Making of Late Antiquity* (Cambridge, MA; Harvard University Press, 1978), 54-80.

icon, the belief is that the person or persons represented in the icon are looking back on us.

We can pray before an icon by praying out loud, or by meditating quietly upon the saint (or saints) they represent, especially when there is a story represented in it through the juxtaposition of image and symbol, or by simply gazing upon the icon itself and commune with those represented there who are pondering us from the other side of the window. Icons are sacramentals which, by their very nature, are oriented toward the divine mysteries, the sacraments, especially the Eucharist, and thus being of a social nature, tend toward the community of the faithful. They unite the individual to the believing community—and vice versa. As such, they represent the Mystical Body of Christ—the Church militant, purgative, and triumphant—a single supernatural organism made up of many members.

As instruments of prayer, icons require the seeds of faith, hope, and love, the three things that last (1 Cor 13:13). They presuppose faith because they are not merely works of art to be appreciated as a this-worldly reality, but also instruments of prayer that require faith in the redemptive mysteries of Christ, so the grace of the Holy Spirit may be unleashed in our souls. They require hope that we may one day pass through the window into the divine before us and enjoy the heavenly realities to which they point, thus enabling them to participate in an even more intimate relation with the Father, Son, and Spirit. Finally, as sacramentals, they make the divine realities to which they point present to us so that the divine love may take root in our lives and daily actions. Since Christ himself represents in his humanity the fullness of faith, hope, and love, he is the icon of God par excellence. When seen in this light, all icons point to Christ and the intimate relation between the divine and human manifest in his life by virtue of the hypostatic union.

Icon of the Father

The hypostatic union (the union of Jesus' divine and human natures) is a supernatural grace, a mystery unfathomable by human reason and unknowable except through divine revelation. It is a *de fide* mystery of faith and dogma of the Church. It states that the mysterious union of Jesus' divine and human natures took place at the moment of his conception in the womb of the Blessed Virgin, that it will never be undone, that each of these natures maintains its own will and mode of operation, while at the same time maintaining Jesus' unique personhood as the one and only Son of the Father, the Second Person of the Blessed Trinity.[2] Because of this mysterious union of the human and divine in the person of Jesus Christ, he himself can be seen as an Icon of the Father. After all, he said, "The Father and I are one" (Jn 10:30) and "I am the way, and the truth, and the life. No one comes to the Father except through me" (Jn 14: 6).[3] When seen as the Icon of the Father, Jesus offers us a window into which we can peer into the very ground of our existence, that reveals to us the truth about life (and about ourselves) and gives us a participation in divine life itself. As St. Athanasius of

---

[2] Ott, *Fundamentals of Christian Dogma*, rev. ed. Robert Fastiggi (Baronius Press, 2020), 162-65.

[3] All quotations from Scripture come from *The Holy Bible: New Revised Standard Version with Apocrypha* (New York: Oxford University Press, 1989).

Alexandria (c. 296/98-373) says, "God became man, so man might become divine."[4]

Christ as been called "the face of the Father's Mercy."[5] When we contemplate his face, he reveals to us our human brokenness and shows us the Father's compassion and forgiveness. He entered our world and became one of us (in the mystery of the Incarnation), gave himself completely to the point of dying for us (in the mystery of his passion and death), to become nourishment for us (in the mystery of the Eucharist), and a source of hope for us (in the mystery of his Resurrection and Ascension to heaven). He did all this because of the Father's love for us. He emptied himself on our behalf because he was one with the Father and he suffered and died for us out of love for the Father and out of love for us. While remaining distinct from his human nature, Jesus' divinity shines through his humanity in a way similar to how the golden background of an icon shines through the clothing and faces of the figures represented in it: Mary, Joseph, John the Baptist, the

---

[4] Athanasius of Alexandria, *On the Incarnation*, 54.3.
[5] Pope Francis, *Misericordiae vultus*, no. 1.

Apostles, the angels, and especially Jesus himself. His divinity enters us and shines through us in a special way whenever we celebrate and receive the Eucharist. For this reason, if Jesus is the Icon of the Father, then the Eucharist is the Icon of Jesus par excellence, for it brings Jesus' glorified humanity into intimate contact with us and gradually conforms our humanity unto his, thus continuing a process of divinization that culminates in our seeing God face-to-face in the beatific vision.

As an Icon of Christ, the Eucharist is a meal commemorating the Last Supper over which he presided, a sacrifice immersing us personally in the one sacrifice of Golgotha in which Jesus himself was the sacrificial Lamb of God, and a presence, whereby his glorified post-resurrectional existence is completely present—body, soul, blood, and divinity—in the consecrated and completely transformed (and transubstantiated) species of bread and wine. The Eucharist brings us into close personal communion with Jesus our Redeemer. When at Mass, we do what he commanded his disciples to do; we remember him in the breaking of the bread. When at Mass, we ourselves share in his suffering and death on the cross.

When at Mass, Jesus is present to us in the person of the priest, in the reading and exposition of God's Word, in the worshiping community, and, in a special way, in the consecrated bread and wine. When receiving Holy Communion, we are united with Jesus' glorified existence, a union that promises over time to turn us into another Christ so that with the Apostle Paul, we to can say, "[I]t is no longer I who live, but it is Christ who lives in me" (Gal 2:20). To gaze upon the Eucharist when the priest after the consecration raises the host and chalice for all to see, or before the monstrance in quiet adoration, is to peer into the awesome mysteries of the Incarnation, Redemption, and untold wonders of the Triune God.

Let It Be Done Unto Me

Some of the most popular Christian icons are those of Mary holding the child Jesus in her arms and looking either down at him or out to us. Mary was Jesus' first and closest disciple. Because of her humble *fiat*—"Here I am, the servant of the Lord; let it be with me according to your word" (Lk 1:38)—which allowed the Incarnation to take place, God has given her a special role in the mystery of redemption and in the history of humanity's ultimate destiny.

Because of her glorious assumption into heaven, Mary alone, out of all humanity, experiences at this very moment the fullness of redemption. Everyone else, is awaiting the resurrection of the dead at Jesus' second coming and at the end of time, but her body has already been assumed into heaven, and she presently enjoys the full fruits of the redemptive process brought about by her son's paschal mystery.

Because she is fully divinized, she sits at her son's right hand as Queen of Heaven and the Mother of the Church, the community of the faithful. St. Thérèse of Lisieux, however, once remarked:

> "We know very well that the Blessed Virgin is Queen of heaven and earth, but she is more Mother than Queen; and we should not say, on account of her prerogatives, that she surpasses all the saints in glory just as the sun at its rising makes the stars disappear from sight. My God! How strange that would be! A mother who makes her children's glory vanish! I myself think just the

> contrary. I believe she'll increase the splendor of the elect very much."[6]

Mary's humility sheds light on her sons and daughters and brings them to the fore. Her one desire is to lead others to her son. She intercedes for us by pleading to him on our behalf. She follows her son very closely, so much so that anyone who wishes to respond to Jesus' call to deny ourselves, take up our crosses daily, and follow him (Lk 9:23) must follow her as well. If Jesus, the Second Adam, reveals to us the fullness of what it means to be fully human, then Mary, the Second Eve, shows us that this possibility has already become a reality in one of us and that we, too, can hope to one day share in Jesus' glorified humanity. That is why in the *Salve Regina* we call her "our life, our sweetness, and our hope." Mary and Jesus are so often depicted together in Christian iconography because he reveals what we are called to become and she reminds us that the fullness of divini-

---

[6] Thérèse of Lisieux, *Her Last Conversations*, trans. John Clarke (Washington, D.C. ICS Publications, 1977), 161.

zation, that mysterious sharing in the divine to which all are called, has already taken place.

The Friends of God

If the Blessed Mother was (and is) Jesus' closest disciple, then the saints follow soon afterward. They are the ones who took his invitation to deny themselves and follow him seriously. They embraced his Gospel message of love and took to heart the new commandment he gave his followers, "I give you a new commandment, that you love one another. Just as I have loved you, you also should love one another" (Jn 13: 34). How they expressed that love varied from situation to situation, in time and place, from one historical period to the next. What they had in common was their faith in Jesus, their Lord, and their desire to follow him and spread his message to the ends of the earth.

As mentioned earlier, the saints were known in the early centuries of the Church as the "friends of God." Much has been written on friendship in the ancient world and in the Christian tradition. In his *Nicomachean Ethics*, Aristotle speaks of three different kinds of friendship: those of utility based on usefulness, those of pleasure, based on enjoyment, and those of character, based on character and the pursual of the good.[7] In his *Summa theologiae*, Thomas Aquinas (1224/25-74) calls charity "a certain type of friendship of man for God."[8] In his *On Spiritual Friendship,* the twelfth-century Cistercian abbot, Aelred of Rievaulx (1110-67) writes of spiritual friendship rooted in Christ.[9] In the Gospel of John, Jesus himself tells his disciples,

> "I do not call you servants any longer, because the servant does not know what his master is doing; but I have called you friends, because I have made known to you everything that I have heard from my Father." (Jn 15:15)

---

[7] Aristotle, *Nicomachean Ethics*, 1156a10-24; 1056b6-22.

[8] Thomas Aquinas, *Summa theologiae*, II-II, q, 23, a. 5, resp.

[9] Aelred of Riveaulx, *Spiritual Friendship,* 1.1.

Chapter One: Jesus Christ: Icon of the Father

Based on Aristotle's analysis of friendship, Christian theologians and spiritual writers have identified specific marks: benevolence (actively seeking the other's well-being), reciprocity (making sure the relationship is mutual), and mutual indwelling (carrying the other in one's heart).[10] C.S. Lewis writes that friends exist side by side, absorbed in some common interest.[11] For Christians, that common interest is Christ. Jesus himself said, "…where two or three are gathered in my name, I am there among them" (Mt 18:20). The saints were called the "friends of God" precisely because they were friends of Christ. They built the kingdom in their little corner of the world by gathering in his name and spreading his love, as a tiny ember sets off a spark and eventually a raging fire. As Jesus once said, "I have come to bring fire to the earth, and how I wish it were already kindled!" (Lk 12:49). Jesus wishes us, too, to be enflamed with the fire off God's love!

---

[10] Aquinas, *Summa theologies,* II-II, q. 23, a. 1, resp.; q. 24, a. 11, resp

[11] C.S. Lewis, *The Four Loves* (San Diego, CA: Harcourt Brace Jovanovich Publishers, 1960), 91.

The Call to Holiness

In chapter five of *Lumen gentium,* the Second Vatican Council's "Dogmatic Constitution on the Church," the Council fathers state: "Therefore all the faithful are invited and obliged to holiness and the perfection of their own state of life."[12] This universal call to holiness is based on Jesus' words, "Be perfect, therefore, as your heavenly Father is perfect" (Mt 5:48), reiterated in the Catechism of the Catholic Church,[13] and found in the writings of many of the great saints of the past who claimed that all men, women, and children are called to holiness by uniting their wills with the Lord's. Saints such as Francis de Sales (1567-1622)[14] and Alphonsus de Liguori (1696-1787),[15] moreover, have specifically stated that all walks of life in the Church are called to holiness.

Given our fallen state and our propensity to sin, this may seem to be a tall order for the ordinary

---

[12] Second Vatican Council, *Lumen gentium*, no. 42.

[13] *Catechism of the Catholic Church*, no. 2013.

[14] Francis de Sales, *Introduction to the Devout Life*, 1.3

[15] Alphonsus de Liguori, *The Practice of the Love of Jesus Christ*, 8.9.

believer. Still, as Jesus once said, "For mortals it is impossible, but for God all things are possible" (Mt 19:26). By virtue of his passion, death, resurrection, and ascension into heaven, Jesus redeemed us of our fallen state so that now we only need to deal with the remnant of our fallen state, what the Church calls concupiscence (or *fomes peccati*). The original sin of our ancestors, in other words, has been forgiven and the outpouring of the Holy Spirit, a consequence of Jesus' triumph in his paschal mystery, empowers us to overcome the tendency to give in to our unruly passions. The three-fold way of purgation, illumination, and union reminds us that the way to holiness is a journey, one that lasts a lifetime and, probably in most cases, even beyond.

God, in other words, wishes everyone to be saved and one day see him face-to-face (1 Tm 2:4-6). Holiness is not a calling of a certain type of Christian but of all believers. There are four states of life within the Catholic Church that offer a way to holiness: priesthood, consecrated life, holy matrimony, and the chaste single life. Each of these states have a specific role to play with Christ's mystical body: the priesthood regulates the proper administration of the sacraments; religious life gives witness to the radical following of Christ by professing the evangelical counsels of chastity, poverty, and obedience; the laity (both married and single) have been commissioned to bring the Gospel into the marketplace, albeit in different ways.

Each of these states of life are united in their sincere desire to follow in the footsteps of Christ. They differ in that, as members of Christ's body, they each serve a different function in the Church: "God has arranged the members in the body, each one of them, as he chose. If all were a single member, where would the body be?" (I Cor 12:18-19). What is more, as the fathers of the Second Vatican Council remind us:

> Those who, through no fault of their own, do not know the Gospel of Christ or his Church, but who nevertheless seek God with a sincere heart, and moved by grace, try in their actions to do his will as they know it through the dictates of their conscience—those too may achieve eternal salvation.[16]

---

[16] Second Vatican Council, *Lumen gentium*, no. 16.

Chapter One: Jesus Christ: Icon of the Father

Conclusion

Jesus is the Icon of God, the face of the Father's Mercy. He is a window into the mystery of the divine, as well as a window into our very selves, revealing to us what it means to be fully human. Being both human and divine, he juxtaposes in his very being both the image and symbol of Christian iconography that enables us to rise out of the downward, catabolic pull of our fallen nature and rise with him in the upward, anabolic pull that ends in his triumph over death and his resurrection and ascension into heaven and our sharing in his glorified humanity and resulting divinization. The Eucharist, in turn, is God's sacramental gift, a veritable Icon of Christ himself, that heralds in this new creation and immerses us in the process by which we ourselves, by eating his body and drinking his blood, gradually become more and more conformed unto him and his glorified humanity.

As Jesus' closest follower, Mary is an Icon of Humanity, someone who in her glorious assumption body and soul into heaven experiences the fullness of redemption that the rest of humanity, even the saints in heaven, still await to happen at the end of time when Jesus returns in his Second Coming to bring the present world as we know it and transform it into something new: "See, I am making all things new" (Rev 21:5). "I am the Alpha and Omega, the first and the last, the beginning and the end" (Rev 22: 13). The saints, in turn, as the "friends of God," whose souls are with God but who still await the resurrection of the dead, are a source of hope for us that, because with God all things are possible, we, too, might one day become worthy of the title and see God face-to-face in the beatific vision.

God wishes everyone to be saved. He created us out of love for us, and he wishes us to love him in return. Jesus entered our world so that we could enter into friendship with him and the intimate love he shares with the Father and Holy Spirit. This universal call to holiness extends to everyone, believers and nonbelievers alike. It manifests itself in different states of life, each of which represents an authentic following of Christ in his mystical body, the Church, which is itself, like Mary her mother, an Icon of Christ through whom all who participate in her life may find their way to the Father and enjoy the fruits of Christ's redemptive action.

Reflection Questions

- Have you ever prayed before an icon? If so, what did you do? What did you say? What did you think? Did you simply gaze into it in silence? How would you describe your experience?
- In what sense is Jesus and icon of God? How does he mediate the Father's presence to those who encounter him? How do you pray to Jesus? What do you share with him? Do you use words? Thoughts? Have you ever simply rested in silence before the Tabernacle or before an icon of him?
- Do you believe that everyone is called to holiness. What does this call mean for priests? For religious and consecrated persons? For laity? What does the call for holiness mean for your particular state in life? Do you have a long way to go to achieve your goal? Do you ask God for help?
- Do you believe in the communion of saints? Do you think of them as the friends of God? Do you have a devotion to anyone in parti-

cular. Do you have a devotion to the Blessed Virgin Mary? How does your devotion to her differ from your devotion to the other saints? How does your devotion to her differ from your worship of God?

- In what sense is the Eucharist an icon of God? How does it mediate God's grace to you? Do you believe that the Eucharist is the body, blood, soul, and divinity of Jesus Christ? Why is it important to receive the Eucharist? How does it bring us closer to Jesus? How does it differ from the other sacraments?

Prayer to the Holy Spirit

Spirit of God, Comforter and Paraclete, come to me and guide me to follow the way of the Lord Jesus. Help me to contemplate him at all times so I live in him and him in me. Give me the grace to turn what I see in him into words and actions. Give me the grace to become a true disciple.

Chapter Two

The Human Person: Icon of Christ

Created in God's image and likeness, human beings are by nature open to the transcendent ground of reality from which all things come: We are "capable of God" (*capax Dei*), and our happiness lies in God alone.

In this chapter, we will take an anthropological approach to the insights drawn in the previous chapter. By looking at the contours of our human makeup, it will be easier for us to both see and understand how we ourselves are veritable "icons of prayer," through whom God's love shines. By contemplating the Christ in both others and ourselves, our hearts can pass through the window of time, commune with Eternity itself, and experience a foretaste of the communion with God which is already here yet-to-come. This eschatological dimension of human existence is embedded in our very nature but highlighted and brought to the fore by the mystery of God's Word becoming flesh. Jesus, who time again said he and his

Father in heaven were one (e.g., Jn 10:30-38), reveals to us the true meaning and purpose of our humanity.

The Voice of the Apostle

The Apostle Paul, known as "The Apostle of the Gentiles" and referred to by Thomas Aquinas simply as "The Apostle," gives in his letters a clear indication of what a sound Christian anthropology entails. The key texts in this regard appear in 1 Thessalonians and 1 Corinthians. Taken together, these texts reveal the physical, intellectual/psychological, spiritual, and social dimensions of human existence.

At the end of 1 Thessalonians, Paul bids farewell to his readers with the following words:

> "May the God of peace himself sanctify you entirely; and may your spirit and soul, and body. Be kept sound and blameless in the coming of our Lord Jesus Christ. The one who calls you is faithful, and he will do this." (1 Th 5:23-24)

This passage offers us a fourfold understanding of the human person as being physical, mental, spiritual, and social. A look at each of these facets of the human person will help us to appreciate more what contemplating the image of Christ in others and ourselves implies.

To begin with, Paul prays that the God of peace may sanctify the Thessalonians in their spirit (*pneuma*). This aspect of human existence represents the depths of the human heart, the place where the Lord himself wishes to dwell. It is the deepest dimension of the human person, that place within the heart where the human spirit can commune with God in a bond of intimate friendship. Next, he wishes that the Lord himself sanctify themselves in their soul (*psyche*). This stands for the mental faculties of the human person that include the rational, volitional, and emotional parts of our existence. It highlights the thinking, willing, and feeling capacities that we have as human beings and which distinguish us qualitatively from the rest of God's creation. He then goes on to ask God to sanctify them in their body (*soma*). This physical dimension of human existence connects us with the material world and distinguishes us from the angelic world. It should also be distinguished from Paul's use of the word "flesh" (*sarx*), which he associates with the sins of the flesh in a fallen world. After reminding the Thessalonians that they are spiritual, intellectual/psychological, and physical beings, Paul, it must be remembered, is addressing them not only as individuals but as a community, the body (*soma*) of Christ. This social dimension of human existence is an integral part of our human makeup that cannot be separated from the other three. Paul expresses his teaching on the Christian community as the "body of Christ" most clearly in 1 Corinthians 12:12, where he states:

> "For just as the body and has many members, and all members of the body, though many, are one body, so it is with Christ. For in the one Spirit we were all baptized into one body—Jew or Greeks, slaves or free—and we were all made to drink of one Spirit." (1 Cor 12:12-13)

The implications of Paul's teachings are clear: We have spiritual, intellectual/psychological, physical, and social dimensions to our human makeup. When we are baptized into the one body of Christ, every aspect of our being is incorporated into Christ who, as the Word-made-flesh, possesses these very same aspects. In baptism, our humanity is immersed into Christ's, and we become divinized by virtue of his humanity's intimate relationship and oneness with his Father in heaven.

The Sin of Human Origins

If God entered our world and became man in the person of Jesus Christ to reveal to us the fullness of our humanity, the question arises: Why did he need to do this in the first place? If God created man in his image and likeness, then why was that not enough to show us who we were and where we were headed. Why, in other words, did God become man (*Cur Deus homo*? as St. Anselm of Canterbury would put it)? The answer to this question has to do with the presence of evil in the world effected by humanity's fall from grace in the mystery of original sin.

According to the *Catechism of the Catholic Church*, "The doctrine of original sin is, so to speak, the 'reverse side' of the Good News that Jesus is the Savior of all men, that all need salvation, and that salvation is offered to all through Christ."[1] It goes on to say that the story of the Fall in the third chapter of Genesis "...uses figurative language, but affirms a primeval event, a deed that took place *at the beginning of the history of man.*"[2] Furthermore, the Church does not consider itself authorized to tamper with this divinely revealed mystery as it has been revealed in God's Word and affirmed by the tradition of the Church. When seen in this light, Jesus reveals to us the fullness of what it means to be human because the image and likeness of God in which we have been created has been deeply wounded as a result of humanity's primal fall from grace. As a result of the sin of Adam and Eve, our minds have become darkened, our wills weakened, and our passions out of sync. Untouched by the effects of original sin, Jesus shows us what it means to be truly human.

Sin, we must remember, is an analogous concept, where there are always likenesses and differences. It

---

[1] *Catechism of the Catholic Church*, no. 390.
[2] Ibid.

has three levels: the universal, social, and personal. Original sin affects all of humanity on the universal level. Social sin is a human creation and pertains to those sinful structures that have become embedded in society. Personal sin is committed by individual human beings and is further divided into mortal and venial sin. The former cuts off our relationship with God and pertains to grave matter done with full knowledge and consent. The latter and has to do with less serious offenses against God and neighbor and allows us to remain in the state of grace. Sin, on all its levels, has an effect on our human dignity, of which there are two levels or dimensions.

The Dignity of the Human Person

Of the two levels of human dignity, one is deeply rooted in human nature and cannot change; the other can increase or decrease, depending on the quality of our actions. The former is immutable because all human beings are created in the image and likeness of God and, regardless of the status of their moral character, will always remain so. The latter can either wax or wane, grow or diminish, depending on whether our actions are good or bad, gracious or sinful. When seen in this light, our human dignity is, at one and the same time, both immutable and mutable, stable and unstable, permanently reflective of God and changeable depending on our virtuous or vicious actions. Let us now take a look at each of these levels of our human dignity.

According to the *Catechism of the Catholic Church*, "Being in the image of God, the human individual possesses the dignity of a person, who is not just something, but someone. He is capable of self-knowledge, of self-possession and of freely giving himself and entering into communion with other persons."[3] This fundamental dignity can never be taken away from us. No matter what we do, whether our actions are good or bad, regardless of how we act, we will for all eternity reflect the image of God by virtue of our very existence. God, our creator, made us in his image in likeness. That is something we cannot change. This is one of the reasons why the Church does not condone capital punishment. Even the most hardened criminal, who has committed the most

---

[3] Ibid., 357.

heinous crime, still reflects God's image in his or her very being. That image may be darkened or clouded over on account of one's vicious actions, but it will always remain and never disappear.

At the same time, the *Catechism* continues, man "…is called by grace to a covenant with his Creator, to offer him a response of faith and love that no other creature can give in his stead."[4] Because God has given us free will, we can cooperate with God's grace or not. We can keep the covenant God made with us or break it. We can live virtuous lives or vicious ones. Because we have the power of free choice, we can allow God's grace to polish the image of God in us so that it reflects the glory of divine light even more, or we can tarnish it and even cover it over with the darkness of our evil actions. Our actions have consequences both in the outer world and our inner world. They have a ripple effect on the world around us but also one that affects our very souls. The choices we make affect this second level of our human dignity. Through them, we can become our truest selves or our false selves. We can, through the help of God's

---

[4] Ibid.

grace, become divinized or, through our desire to go our own way and make ourselves the center of the moral universe, sink into the lower realms of our animal nature and dwell in darkness we call hell.

Human Dignity and Catholic Social Doctrine

The dignity of the human person lies at the very heart of the Church's social teaching. As John Paul II points out, it

> …is manifested in all its radiance when the person's origin and destiny are considered: created by God in his image and likeness as well as redeemed by the most precious blood of Christ, the person is called to be a 'child in the Son' and a living temple of the Spirit, destined for eternal life of blessed communion with God.[5]

When seen in this light, our dignity is ultimately rooted in God's love for us. God created us out of

---

[5] John Paul II, *Christifideles laici,* no. 37.

love, redeemed us when we went astray, and now transforms us through life in the Spirit. He did all of this so we might enjoy entering an intimate communion with him, a union of divine friendship.

The Church's teaching on human dignity has sometimes been misconstrued in a way that emphasizes only the permanent, unchangeable dimension of human dignity to the exclusion of its changeable character. According to J. Brian Benestad, "…it may be more reasonable to proclaim both the permanent character of human dignity as well as the obligation to ennoble one's dignity by a life of holiness, *with the help of divine grace*."[6] The permanent and changeable dimensions of human dignity go hand in hand and should not be separated. Benestad goes on to cite John Paul II's understanding of human dignity and its relationship to democracy: "People perfect their dignity by using their freedom to live as they ought, and by doing so they contribute to the smooth functioning of a healthy democracy."[7]

---

[6] J. Brian Benestad, *Church, State, and Society: An Introduction to Catholic Social Doctrine* (Washington, D.C.: The Catholic University off America Press, 20100), 43.

[7] Ibid., 44.

The connection between the dignity of the human person and the well-being of society evokes the notion of microcosm/macrocosm and the intimate relationship shared by them. According to this notion, human society represents the soul writ large. The outer world is a projection of the inner world. A virtuous society is possible only when its members strive to live virtuously. The dignity of human society is thus a function of the dignity of its citizens. Since they possess a two-fold dignity (one permanent; the other changeable), it follows that society itself has by analogy something very similar. The societies we create are expressions of our social nature and tell us something about ourselves.

A Spirituality of Communion

Because human beings are imperfect, the societies they build are dysfunctional (although some more than others). Even families, the basic building blocks of society are, to one degree or another, out of sync and slightly dysfunction. "There is only one holy family," as the saying goes: Jesus, Mary, and Joseph. This state of imperfection is because we live in a fallen world. As pointed out earlier, the Church's doctrine of original sin describes in figurative language a sense deeply rooted in our hearts that something had gone awry in our ancient past and that we are suffering the consequences of that fateful flaw to this day. The sin of human origins, however, is only part of the human story. It must be complemented by the selfless love of the Redeeming Christ and the sanctifying work of the Spirit. We were created not to wallow in our imperfections but to lives of holiness made possible by the grace of the Holy Spirit, what Thomas Aquinas calls the "Law of the Gospel" or the "Evangelical Law."[8]

During our earthly sojourn, we live in a world of imperfection but as Christians believe we are headed to our heavenly homeland, where whatever is lacking in our human nature will be filled with the fullness of divine grace. In that Somewhere, which some call Paradise and which Myles Connolly in the person of Mr. Blue calls the "Tavern at the End of the World,"[9]

---

[8] Thomas Aquinas, *Summa theologiae*, I-II, q. 106, a. 1, resp.

[9] Myles Connolly, *Mr. Blue* (Garden City, NY: Image Books, 1954), 76.

there will be no sin and imperfection because holiness will reign. Jesus himself once said, "Be perfect, therefore, as your heavenly Father is perfect" (Mt 5:48). In this present life, we live with one foot in this world and the other in the next. In the words of Augustine, we live in the "City of Man" but are making or way to the "City of God."[10] For this reason, we are all "strangers in a foreign land." In fact, the words "parish," "parishioner," and 'parochial" all come from the Greek work, *paroikia* which precisely means that![11]

Our human destiny is to be members of that perfect society known as the Communion of Saints. The destiny of the Church militant (those here on earth) and the Church purgative (those who are died and are going through a process of purgation) is to arrive in our heavenly homeland and live in a New Creation in communion with God and all those who have left

---

[10] Augustine of Hippo, *De civitate Dei*, 1.1.1.

[11] Walter Bauer, *A Greek-English Lexicon of the New Testament and Other Early Christian Literature,* trans. and eds. William F. Arndt and F. Wilbur Gingrich, 2d ed. (Chicago: University of Chicago Press, 1979), s. v. "παροικία."

this earth marked with the sign of faith. We will become members of the Communion of Saints and enjoy the "vision of God" (*visio Dei*) for all eternity. During our earthly pilgrimage, we can anticipate the coming of the kingdom and receive a foretaste of the heavenly banquet by living out to the best of our ability the spirituality of communion. John Paul II describes it in this way:

> A spirituality of communion indicates above all the heart's contemplation of the mystery of the Trinity dwelling in us, and whose light we must also be able to see shining on the face of the brothers and sisters around us. A spirituality of communion also means an ability to think of our brothers and sisters in faith within the profound unity of the Mystical Body, and therefore as "those who are a part of me." This makes us able to share in their joys and sufferings, to sense their desires and attend to their needs, to offer them deep and genuine friendship. A spirituality of communion also implies the ability to see what is positive in others, to welcome it and prize it

as a gift from God; not only as a gift for the brother or sister who has received it directly, but also as a "gift for me." A spirituality of communion means, finally, to know how to "make room" for our brothers and sisters, bearing "each other's burdens" (Gal 6:2) and resisting the selfish temptations which constantly beset us and provoke competition, careerism, distrust and jealousy. Let us have no illusions: unless we follow this spiritual path, external structures of communion will serve very little purpose. They would become mechanisms without a soul, 'masks' of communion rather that its means of expression and growth.[12]

Such is the path we are all called to walk.

Conclusion

Each of us is a living icon, an image of God, a window that opens to eternity through which we can

---

[12] John Paul II, *Novo Millennio Ineunte*, no. 43.

Chapter Two: The Human Person: Icon of Christ

encounter our Maker, the Divine Artist, who brought us into being and who keeps us in being, day by day, year by year, moment by moment. Fallen creatures as we are, the image of God implanted in our very being can never be erased. At the same time, our thoughts and actions influence the way we reflect God's image to the world. When we cooperate with God's grace and live virtuously, the light of the Divine shines through us and we become living bearers of the Word, living Christs in the spirit of the Apostle, Paul, who said, "…it is no longer I who live, but it is Christ who lives in me" (Gal 2:20).

During our earthly sojourn, there will always be a gap between where we are and where God wants us to be. The question each of us must ask ourselves is if that gap is getting larger or smaller. Our response to that question will give some indication as to where our destiny lies. The choice before each of us is stark: cooperate with God's grace, or not. There is no alternative, no other option. If we remain open to the grace of the Spirit, we will one day reach our journey's end and behold the face of the Lord, whose brilliant light will shine through the image in whom we were made in all its divine glory. If we do not, we will be set adrift for all eternity in a sea of our own private wants and needs, left to ourselves to fill a hole deep within our soul with what ultimately can be filled, not by any earthly riches, goods, or desires, but by only God himself.

We are all made in the image and likeness of God. That image is implanted within us and forms a part of our very nature. Although it cannot be destroyed, it can be shined and polished by the way we live our lives. The choice to do so remains before each of us. We can become virtuous or vicious people. We can allow the Spirit of the Lord our God to dwell within our hearts and become our deepest, truest selves, or we can live our lives pursuing a false, empty goal of our own making, which will lead to nothing more than passing pleasures. The choice is ours to make. Who we are and what we will become depends on our freedom to choose to befriend our befriending God—or not.

Reflection Questions

- How would you describe the various dimensions of our human makeup? Which of them do you feel most comfortable with? Which of them do you have a difficult time relating to? Are these various dimensions integrated in your life? How do they challenge you to do you believe grow?

- What are the various levels of human dignity? Do you believe you were created in the image and likeness of God? Is that a dignity that can never be taken away from you? Is there another level of dignity that can wax or wane depending on how we live? How does our dignity suffer when we sin and lead vicious lives? How does it grow when we live virtuously?

- Do you believe you are an icon of Christ? If so, how can you best mediate his presence to others? Can you do this by yourself? Do you need God's help? What can you do to receive God's help? In what way does the grace of the Spirit help you to reflect Christ's image to others?

- Do you believe you are a stranger in a foreign land? Do you believe that you are on a pilgrim journey with one foot in the City of Man and the other in the City of God? How do you live with the tension of having one foot in two worlds? What can you do to help prepare this present world for its transformation in the next?

- What is the spirituality of communion? What does it entail? How would you describe it? How can we live in communion with Christ? What must we do? How can we deepen our communion with Christ? How can we let it weaken or perhaps lose it altogether? What role does prayer play in maintaining our communion with Christ and others?

Prayer to the Holy Spirit

Spirit of the Living God, lead me to a deeper understanding of myself. Help me to understand what it means for me to be an icon of Christ. Help me to discover what it means for me to be created in the image and likeness of God. Help me to mediate your grace, the life of the Lord Jesus himself to others.

Chapter Three

Contemplating the Human Person

God is an unfathomable, ever-elusive mystery known to us only through his decision to reveal himself to us in time and space. Since God is Existence itself,[1] it follows that existence, too, is unfathomable mystery, known by virtue of our own existence and yet unknown because of our limited experience of it. Since God is love (1 Jn 4:8), it also follows that love itself is similarly both a mystery and yet something known to us by virtue of our being created in the image and likeness of God (Gn 1:26-27). As such, we ourselves are, on a lesser but nonetheless significant scale, mysterious beings who reflect in our own lives the mystery of God himself and the love he bears for us and all his creation.

God is fully known only to himself. What we know of him was made known to us because he revealed himself to us out of love in the person of Jesus

---

[1] Thomas Aquinas, *Summa theologiae*, I, q. 3, a. 4, resp.

Christ. Jesus, in turn, is fully known only to himself, the Father, and the Spirit, the bond of love between them. As Jesus once said, "The Father and I are one" (Jn 10:30). Who Jesus is and what he stands for cannot be pinned down to a single level of meaning. His significance for our lives cannot be confined to a theological formulation. God's revelation conceals as much as it reveals (perhaps even more). The cataphatic (positive theology) is offset by the apophatic (negative theology). What we know is dwarfed by what we do not know of him. To us, he remains, at one and the same time, both revealed and hidden, known and unknown, human and divine. Even though he reveals to us the fullness of our humanity, even that remains partially hidden from us since there will always be more of it to discover. Like Jesus, but on a lesser scale, we ourselves cannot be reduced to a single level of meaning. As physical, intellectual/psychological, spiritual, and social beings, we are fully known to God alone. We have only limited knowledge of ourselves. We know ourselves in part and are always discovering more about ourselves in relation to ourselves, God, and others. The question we will examine in this chapter is: How do we understand the human person? What, in other words, are the interpretive lenses through which we can arrive at a proper understanding of our own self-understanding? To do so, we will align the anthropological dimensions outlined in the previous chapter with the Church's understanding of the various senses of Scripture.

The Philosophical Backdrop

As seen in chapter two, there are physical, intellectual/psychological, spiritual, and social dimensions to our human makeup. These line up well with the fourfold senses of Scripture listed in the *Catechism of the Catholic Church*: the literal, the allegorical, the moral (tropological), and the anagogical.[2] Before explaining each of these senses and aligning them with the anthropological dimensions of our human makeup, it would be helpful to examine their philosophical underpinnings, which have their roots in Platonism and, in a particular way, the Neo-

---

[2] *Catechism of the Catholic Church*, nos. 116-17.

platonic Church fathers such as Augustine adapted and integrated into the Catholic faith.

While Platonists generally believed that reality consisted in a world of Ideal Forms and the visible reality was nothing but a vague reflection of that higher, invisible realm, Neoplatonists said the physical world resulted in a series of emanations from the One, the Divine Mind (Nous), and the World Soul. The physical sensible world, in turn, emanated from this Divine Triad of Being, Mind, and Spirit. In adapting Neoplatonic thought to Christianity, Augustine identified this Triad with the doctrine of the Trinity: The One was the Father; the Divine Mind, the Son; the World Soul, the Spirit. In addition, he did away with the notion of emanation, which carried with a sense of divine necessity, and replaced with that of creation, which God does freely and not out of necessity. The visible world is thus seen as a creation of God the Father that exists in the Logos or Divine Mind of the Son and participates in the world of ideas through the power of the Spirit.

The belief that these Forms (or Universals) are Ideas in the Mind of God and are the basis of all visible reality had a great effect on how the Church fathers interpreted the Scriptures. Since the Gospels were written in common (*koine*) Greek and, even in their Latin translation, were not known as literary masterpieces, the fathers of the Church tried to delve beneath the surface of the text and look for patterns that corresponded with other ideas either in the text itself or the teachings of the Church, patterns that corresponded to the Ideas in the Mind of the Divine Logos. In doing so, they found a way to discover rich theological, moral, and spiritual meaning in a text which on the surface seemed to have little (if any) spiritual value for the reader.

This search for meaning beneath the literal meaning of the text led people like Augustine to view the Scriptures as rife with spiritual meaning and enabled them to interpret the Scriptures with a heightened sense of awareness that the Spirit of God was using the Scriptures to touch their minds and hearts and give them deep insight into their relationship with God and the direction of their spiritual journey. Augustine's view was held by many: "For now treat the Scripture of God as the face of God. Melt in its presence."[3]

Given this philosophical mindset, the search for the spiritual senses of the text would not be considered eisegesis (reading *into* the text), as proponents of the historical critical method would tend to say, but genuine exegesis, in the sense that they are drawing out meaning from the text, meaning that is in the text but hidden from plain sight. The nature of true exegesis depends on the philosophical presuppositions held by the interpreter and embedded in the method used. Historical critical exegesis generally presupposes a nominalist approach, which denies the existence of universals and believes in the existence of particulars alone. The Neoplatonic approach to Scripture, by way of contrast, affirms universal ideas as the basis of reality and that there are hidden patterns beneath the literal meaning of the text that put the reader in touch with them. The fact that the Church recognizes the importance of both indicates

---

[3] Augustine of Hippo, *Sermons*, 22.7. Cited in Robert Louis Wilken, *The Spirit of Early Christian Thought* (New Haven: Yale University Press, 2003), 50.

that both approaches could (and should) be used in conjunction with one another. Still, as Thomas Aquinas suggests, the spiritual senses of Scripture must flow from the literal and all sound theological argument must be drawn from it alone.[4] The Pontifical Biblical Commission affirms something very similar: "It is not only legitimate, but it is also absolutely necessary to seek to define the precise meaning of texts as produced by their authors—what is called the 'literal' meaning."[5]

The Senses of Scripture

With this philosophical background in place, we are now in a position to examine the four senses of Scripture as laid out in the *Catechism of the Catholic Church* (1992) and further developed by the Pontifical Biblical Commission's *Interpreting the Bible in the Church* (1993).

As the *Catechism* states,

---

[4] Aquinas, *Summa theologiae*, I, q.1, a. 10, ad 1m.
[5] The Pontifical Biblical Commission, *The Interpretation of the Bible in the Church (Vatican City State: Libreria Editrice Vaticana, 1993)*, 78.

According to an ancient tradition, one can distinguish between two senses of Scripture: the literal and the spiritual, the latter being subdivided into the allegorical, moral, and anagogical senses. The profound concordance of the four senses guarantees all its richness to the living reading of Scripture in the Church.[6]

Let us examine each of these senses one by one.

The Literal Sense. The *Catechism* describes the literal sense as "…the meaning conveyed by the words of Scripture and discovered by exegesis, following the rules of sound interpretation: All other senses of Sacred Scripture are based on the literal."[7] The Pontifical Biblical Commission develops this thought further: "The literal sense of Scripture is that which has been expressed directly by the inspired human authors. Since it is the fruit of inspiration, this sense is also intended by God, as principal author. One arrives at this sense by means of a careful analy-

---

[6] *Catechism of the Catholic Church*, no. 115.
[7] Ibid., no. 116.

sis of the text, within its literary and historical context."[8]

The Allegorical Sense. Through this sense, the *Catechism* states: "We can acquire a more profound understanding of events by recognizing their significance in Christ; thus, the crossing of the Red Sea is a sign or type of Christ's victory and also of Christian Baptism."[9] The Pontifical Biblical Commission, in turn, says:

> Recourse to allegory stems also from the conviction that the Bible, as God's book, was given by God to his people, the Church. In principle, there is nothing in it which is to be set side. As out of date or completely lacking meaning. God is constantly speaking to his Christian people a message that is ever relevant for their time.[10]

---

[8] The Pontifical Biblical Commission, *The Interpretation of the Bible in the Church*, 79.

[9] *Catechism of the Catholic Church*, no. 117.

[10] The Pontifical Biblical Commission, *The Interpretation of the Bible in the Church*, 96.

The Moral Sense. Regarding this sense, the *Catechism* states: "The events reported in Scripture ought to lead us to act justly. As St. Paul says, they were written 'for our instruction.'"[11] It reveals to us something about our souls and the virtues we need to help us walk the path of righteousness. As the Pontifical Biblical Commission points out, as one of the spiritual senses, it is "…the meaning expressed by the biblical texts when read, under the influence of the Holy Spirit, in the context of the paschal mystery of Christ and the new life which flows from it."[12]

The Anagogical Sense. According to the *Catechism*, with this sense: "We can view realities and events in terms of their eternal significance, leading us toward our true homeland: thus, the Church on earth is a sign of the Heavenly Jerusalem."[13] This sense points us in the direction of the four last things: Death, Judgment, Heaven, and Hell. As a spiritual sense, the Pontifical Biblical Commission affirms: "Those who are open to the dynamic aspect of a text

---

[11] *Catechism of the Catholic Church*, no. 117.

[12] The Pontifical Biblical Commission, *The Interpretation of the Bible in the Church*, 81.

[13] *Catechism of the Catholic Church*, no. 117.

will recognize here a profound element of continuity as well as a move to a different level: Christ rules forever, but not on an earthly throne."[14]

Augustine of Denmark describes the four senses in this way: "The literal teaches us history; the allegorical what to believe; the moral how to act; and the anagogical what to hope for."[15] Using this method of interpretation, the word "Jerusalem," which appears numerous times in the Bible, can refer to the city in ancient Israel (literal), the Church (allegorical), the human soul (moral), or the heavenly Jerusalem (anagogical).

An Anthropological Alignment

We are now in a position to align the various dimensions of our human makeup— the physical, the intellectual/psychological, the spiritual, and the social— with the four senses of Scripture. The resulting alignment will give us an interpretative lens through

---

[14] The Pontifical Biblical Commission, *The Interpretation of the Bible in the Church*, 81.

[15] Ibid., 78.

which we can contemplate each human person as a window into eternity, a veritable icon of God that opens up to the transcendent.

The Physical. The bodily dimension of the human person correlates to the literal sense of Scripture. Recall that the Pauline word for "body" (*soma*) has a positive (or at least neutral) connotation, as opposed to his use of the word "flesh" (*sarx*) with its negative association with sins of the flesh. This facet of human existence corresponds with the literal sense, for it roots the human person in time and space. Contemplating others on this level involves considering not only physical appearance, but also their personal history (family, health, language, nationality, marital status, education, work, culture, political views, etc.), in short, everything that has shaped them over the course of their lives. It has to do with what we can know about them through empirical observation and relates to the literal sense of Scripture in that it presents us with the wide range of external information that can be gathered about them.

The Intellectual/Psychological. This dimension of our human makeup pertains to the moral (tropological) sense. It pertains to how we act in the world, whether we live virtuous or vicious lives, whether we strive to live a life of holiness or one of selfishness and sin. Since there is often a gap between where God wants us to be and where we actually are at any given point, the key question to ask here is whether the gap is getting large or smaller. What is more, since action flows from being, it follows that this level will also tell us something about the person's inner intellectual/psychological life. The Greek word used by Paul for "soul" (*psyche*) pertains to our mental capacities of reason, will, memory and imagination, as well as our feelings and emotions, in short, all that comprises our conscious awareness and all that is even on the brink of it. Contemplating others in this way enables us to sense something about their inner lives and the effect it has on their physical existence.

The Spiritual. This dimension of our human makeup relates to the allegorical sense of Scripture. It is concerned with what the person tells us about Christ and his Church. Jesus calls us to friendship and seeks to dwell in our hearts. He accomplishes this by sending his Spirit to commune with our spirits to form an intimate relationship between the divine and the human. Paul's word for "spirit" (*pneuma*) stands for the deepest dimension of the human person, that place which is most open to the transcendent and able to commune with the divine. Because we are "capable of God" (*capax Dei*), we are able to enjoy a relationship with him in a way that no other creature can (not even the angels in heaven). When contemplating others in this way, we receive insights into their relationship with Christ and his Church. We become aware of whether they have a personal relationship with Christ and, if so, how they live out that relationship within the Church.

The Social. This dimension of our human makeup relates to the anagogical sense of Scripture and points to the eternal and our final end in God. In baptism, we are immersed in Christ's paschal mystery: his passion, death, resurrection, and ascension into heaven. In baptism, we are also become members of his body, the Church, and hope one day to see God face-to-face in the beatific vision. As St. Augustine once said, "O Lord…you have made us for yourself, and our hearts are restless until they can find rest in you."[16] We are a pilgrim people on a spiritual journey from the City of Man to the City of God. What is more, we are saved primarily as a people and then as individuals, the implication being that we are all brothers and sisters in Christ and that he himself looks upon us as members of his family. When contemplating others on this level of their human makeup, we see them in light of the last things—death, judgment, heaven, hell—and their final destiny and end in God. Doing so enables us to see them in a different light, as the sons and daughters of God on a journey that, through Christ, will hopefully one day end in the vision of God (*visio Dei*) himself.

This anthropological alignment with the four senses of Scripture gives us a helpful interpretative lens through which we can contemplate those around us on various levels. The union of the various dimensions of our human makeup with the four senses of Scripture gives us a useful contemplative tool that will enable us to see others through the eyes of faith and life in the Spirit. As Paul himself reminds us, "…we walk by faith, not by sight" (2 Cor 5:7).

---

[16] Augustine of Hippo, *The Confessions*, 1.1.

Conclusion

This chapter has sought to develop an interpretative tool to help us ponder ourselves and others and in contemplative manner. By aligning the various dimensions of our human makeup with the four senses of Scripture, we are able to integrate word and image in a way that deepens our encounter with others and fosters in us a contemplative outlook on life. Created in the image and likeness of God, we are living icons, windows to eternity capable of fostering in ourselves and others a deeper relationship with Christ. By using this method of contemplating others, we can appreciate more deeply the mystery of the human person and become more deeply aware of their status as sons and daughters of God.

This anthropological alignment of the four senses of Scripture unites God's creation with God's revelation and enables us to view both in a deeper light. It also enables us to appreciate more deeply the intimate union of word and sacrament that lies at the very heart of Catholic spirituality. If Christ is the sacrament of God and the Church the sacrament of Christ, it follows that we, as the members of Christ's body, share in the Church's sacramentality through our baptism and by leading holy, virtuous lives. When we cooperate with God's grace, we become visible mediators of God's grace to others. Viewing others as icons of Christ helps us to see them as living windows of prayer that deepen our faith, lead us into the beyond, and foster our relationship with ourselves, others, and Christ.

Authentic prayer requires grace and is a human and divine action, involving both God and man. Everyone receives sufficient grace to pray.[17] God's offer of grace is abundant and extends to everyone to either accept or reject. When accepted in our minds and hearts, it leads to the fullness redemption. When rejected, it darkens the image imprinted in us from the moment of our creation. When we look on others as living icons, we have at our disposal a powerful way of seeing how God mysteriously calls each of us to a life of holiness so he can draw us to himself, embrace us, and live in our hearts. He also calls us to befriend one another, so that the life in the Spirit may

---

[17] Alphonsus de Liguori, *Prayer, The Great Means of Salvation,* 2.4.1.

be mutually shared, so that we might help one another walk along the way of holiness.

Reflection Questions

- Do you believe the human person is a mystery who can reveal meanings that delve below the surface? Do you believe that you can contemplate the people around you and find meanings there concerning Christ, the Church, the human soul, human action, and human destiny?
- Do you believe that the senses of Scripture can be applied to the human person and that by using them as interpretative lenses with which to contemplate those around us you can find various levels of meaning in their being created in the image and likeness of God?
- Do you agree that an anthropological alignment can be drawn between these various senses and the dimensions of our human makeup: the physical, intellectual/psychological, spiritual, and social? Have you ever tried contemplating others in this way?

- Can you see yourself using this anthropological alignment? If not, why not? If so, what have you learned about yourself and the faith? Has it deepened your understanding of the incarnational nature of the Christian faith? How has it changed your understanding of what it means to encounter yourself and others?
- Has this approach to contemplating others given you a deeper appreciation of the human person as a living icon of Christ? To what extent has it helped you understand the meaning of Jesus' words, "Truly I tell you, just as you did not do it to one of the least of these, you did not do it to me" (Mt 25:45).

Prayer to the Holy Spirit

Holy Spirit, Advocate, help me to approach others with a contemplative attitude. Help me to ponder them on the various levels of their human makeup. Help me to find meaning in these levels. Help me to celebrate their being created in God's image and likeness. Give me the grace to look upon them as icons of Christ who can draw me closer to the Lord of their lives and mine.

Chapter Four

Befriending the Human Person

As we have seen in previous chapters, God wishes each of us to share a life of intimate friendship with him. We have also seen that the Second Vatican Council reminds us of the universal call to holiness and that salvation comes through Christ alone. The latter does not mean that we must have a conscious recognition of the truths of the Catholic faith. On the contrary, all people of good will and who follow the light of conscience implanted deep within their hearts will be welcomed to God's kingdom with open hearts.[1] Moreover, since we are all called to holiness, it follows that we relate to God not only as individuals but also as a people. When asked what was the greatest of the commandments, Jesus answered, "You shall love the Lord your God with all your heart, and with all your soul, and with all your strength, and with all your mind; and your neighbor as yourself" (Lk 10:27). Loving one another, in

---

[1] Second Vatican Council, *Lumen Gentium.*, no. 16.

other words, is another way of expressing our love for God. He wishes not only to befriend us but also for us to befriend one another. In doing so, we walk together as pilgrims along the road to salvation and life in the heavenly kingdom.

The grace of the Holy Spirit, what Aquinas calls the essence of the "Law of the Gospel,"[2] is given to us all. "Everyone receives sufficient grace to pray," as Alphonsus de Liguori reminds us.[3] If we pray, we will become holy, receive the beatific vision, and live in the presence of God. If we don't pray, we will spend eternity trying to fill a huge hole within our hearts with all sorts of things that, in the end, can only be filled by God himself. We are called to befriend both God and one another. Unfortunately, we live in a world where the word "friend" has become so overused that it has almost become devoid of content. Aristotle, we recall, talks about three types of friendship: utility, pleasure, and character. The Christian tradi-

---

[2] Thomas Aquinas, *Summa theologiae, I-II, q. 106, a. 1, resp.*

[3] St. Alphonsus of Liguori, *Prayer, the Great Means of Salvation*, 1.1.32. See also the *Catechism of the Catholic Church*, no. 2744.

tion has baptized the notion of a friendship of character, or the good, and associated it with friendship with Christ and, through it, the Triune God himself.

This chapter looks specifically at what it means to befriend another person. Its goal is to point out some of the things we can do to foster friendship in a largely friendless world. It seeks to show us how we can find Christ in those around us and, in doing so, fulfill our small but irreplaceable role in building up the kingdom.

Freedom and Holiness

Friendship in Christ is not exclusive and inward looking but oriented toward others and fundamentally open to them. It involves the mutual search for holiness and freedom, both of which reach their fullest expression in friendship with Christ. Along with natural affection (*storge*), romantic love *(*eros*),* selfless love (*agape*), friendship (*philia*) is one of the four loves of the ancient world identified by C.S. Lewis, a professor of Medieval and Renaissance literature, and one of the great popular lay theologians and apologists of the twentieth century.[4] Unlike the natural affection of a mother for her child, or the captivating erotic madness of romantic love, or the heroic self-emptying (*kenosis*) of Christ's death on the cross, friendship, as we have seen earlier, involves two people drawn together by a common interest. In the case of Christians, that interest is the love of Christ and life in the Spirit. All four of these loves, we must remember, are one in God. He looks upon us with fatherly affection (*storge*), is madly in love with us as a lover for his beloved (*eros*), no longer calls us servants but friends (*philia*), and became one of us and gave up his life for us so that we might spend eternity with him (*agape*). What we experience in this world in only a fragmentary way, we will one day experience in the fullness of love though our shared life with him.

To share the friendship of Christ with another person lies at the root of our quest for holiness. This entails nothing other than being filled with the grace of the Holy Spirit and being led by his inner prompt-

---

[4] See C.S. Lewis, *The Four Loves*, (New York: Harcourt, 1991), 41-179.

ings, so that we manifest in our lives his manifold gifts and fruits. Unfortunately, many people today have false notions of what holiness is. For some, it represents a strict puritanical (almost Pelagian) adherence to a rigid moral code, one that demands Herculean efforts to live out and, as a result, invites moral failure and feelings of guilt and judgment for their unworthiness. For others, it stands for God's grace covering our human wretchedness, cloaking it, if you will, but not effecting in us an inner transformation of our lives so that we might truly stand before God as his divinized sons and daughters. Between these two extremes lie a host of other misconceptions and false notions of holiness. Before we can begin to travel the road of true holiness, these false ideas must be struck down and done away with. Only by doing so will we be able to freely embrace Jesus' call to discipleship and his call to live in him and live in the Spirit.

The search for holiness, moreover, is intimately connected with the search for freedom. Jesus once said to the Jews who had believed in him, "If you continue in my word, you are truly my disciples; and you will know the truth, and the truth will make you free"

(Jn 8:31-32). To be a disciple of Christ means that he will lead you not only along the path of holiness but also to experience what it means to be truly free. Like holiness, however, many people today also have false notions of what freedom entails. Some, for example, embrace the radical notion of what Servais Pinckaers calls the "freedom of indifference," a concept popularized by William of Ockham, an early fourteenth-century Franciscan theologian, who posited that freedom lies primarily in the will and not in reason. In his mind, to be truly free a person must be able at all times to choose between two opposites, one thing and its exact contrary. To be influenced by any internal (such a reason) or external force (human law and even divine law) would mitigate one's freedom. The only reason why we should follow God's law is because he is omnipotent and threatens us with eternal damnation if we refuse to obey him. This extreme notion gave rise to moral voluntarism, a dangerous concept that has had a great influence on the development of Catholic moral thought, forcing it to focus on law and one's obligation before the law rather

Chapter Four: Befriending the Human Person

than the quest for virtue and life in the Spirit.[5] For others, freedom involves what Pinckaers refers to as the "freedom for excellence," a focus on striving to be free to do the good and which, for Christianity, involves serving God through life lived in the Spirit.[6] This approach to freedom does not focus on the ability to choose between contraries but to learn the skill of doing what is good. It views the will as fundamentally oriented toward the good presented to it by reason. Rather than focusing on law and obligation, it seeks to acquire those virtues and gifts that will empower us to choose what is good at all times. It welcomes those inner and outer helps such as the infused virtues and the grace and gifts of the Spirit.

Of course, given the fallen nature of the world in which we live, the quest for holiness and true freedom involves a long process of inner conversion. Just as a musician becomes a virtuoso through the hard work of learning to read music and practicing long

---

[5] Pinckaers, Servais, O.P. *The Sources of Christian Ethics*, trans Sr. Mary Thomas Noble, O.P. (Washington, D.C.: The Catholic University of America Press, 1995), 327-53.

[6] Ibid., 354-78.

hours and from playing simple tunes with the music before his or her eyes, to more complicated tunes, to being able to play very complex tunes with the music memorized, to ultimately playing spontaneously and even improvising, so, too, the true disciple embarks on a journey involving the three-fold way of purgation, illumination, and union, which respectively focus on the law, the life of virtue, and being led by the promptings of the Spirit. External promptings such as the law are internalized through the life of virtue and eventually become spontaneous through life in the Spirit. The goal of all this is happiness which, for Christians, means the *visio Dei*, seeing God face-to-face in the beatific vision. The process of conversion represented by the threefold way is not a linear process in which one stage is left behind before going on to the next, but an upward spiraling process where the upward moving process of purgation, illumination, and union gets increasingly smaller and smaller until all three converge to a single point of union with God. Holiness, in other words, leads to true freedom. True freedom, in turn, leads to true happiness, the kind that the world cannot give.

Chapter Four: Befriending the Human Person

An Anthropological Alignment

If happiness stems from our quest for holiness and the freedom to do the good, it reaches its fullness when it permeates every aspect of our being: the physical, the intellectual/psychological, the spiritual, and the social. For this reason, there should be an anthropological alignment on each of these levels. Such an alignment, however, does not merely happen. It often takes a lifetime (and even more) for us to integrate our quest for happiness with every aspect of our being. Let us take a look at what this might mean for us in the nitty gritty, the warp and woof, of everyday life.

The Physical. Our bodies are not something merely accidental to our identity but an integral aspect of who we are. How we treat our bodies says a great deal about ourselves. If we love our bodies, we will take care of them by eating and drinking properly, exercising, and getting enough sleep. If we dislike (or even abhor) our bodies, we will mistreat them by overindulging ourselves with harmful habits that will disfigure them and ultimately do them serious harm. Our bodies are a precious gift from God.

Although they have been ravaged by the effects of humanity's original fall from grace, they have been redeemed by the blood of Christ's death on the cross and are destined to share in his glorified humanity in the world to come. Our bodies are integral to our identity. The choice is ours to either care for them or abuse them. It is wrong to treat them as a superficial add-on to our inner lives. We are not ghosts imprisoned in our bodies but embodied spirits whose DNA reveals something about our deepest, truest selves. What we do to our bodies, how we treat them, what we do with them, tells us something about who we are and where we are going. Our physical existence cannot be separated from the other dimensions of our existence. To do so would be to fall into a brand of Gnosticism that denigrates the material world and relegates our bodies to the periphery of our human makeup.

The Intellectual/Psychological. Our quest for happiness also has implications for our souls, the intellectual/psychological dimensions of our being. Because of original sin, we live in a fallen world. As a result, our minds are darkened, our wills weakened, and our passions distorted and out of sync. We now

Chapter Four: Befriending the Human Person   75

find ourselves in a position where we can either cooperate with Christ's redeeming grace made possible by the gift of his Spirit or give in to the downward pull of sin and corruption. If we cooperate with the grace of the Spirit, our minds will be enlightened, our wills strengthened, and our passions healed and brought in accord with the gentle rule of reason's reign. In this life, there will always be a gap between God's vision of whom he has called us to become and where we are in the present moment. The key question we need to ask ourselves is whether that gap is getting larger or smaller. In other words, we can choose to participate in the anabolic, upward pull of true discipleship and life in the Spirit or in the downward catabolic pull that leads to corruption and death. Our reason, our will, our passions were created to participate in the former. If we give in to the latter, we are not responding to the Spirit's call within our hearts to become our deepest, truest selves. On the contrary, doing so will place us under the power of the Evil One and we will descend into the kingdom of darkness rather than ascend into the Spirit's kingdom of light.

The Spiritual. The human spirit resides in the deepest recesses of the heart and is the place where the Spirit of God encounters us. The Apostle Paul describes this encounter thusly:

> …all who are led by the Spirit of God are children of God. For you did not receive a spirit of slavery to fall back into fear, but you have received a spirit of adoption. When we cry, 'Abba! Father!' it is that very Spirit bearing witness with our spirit that we are children of God, and if children, then heirs, heirs of God and joint heirs with Christ—if, in fact, we suffer with him so that we may also be glorified with him. (Rom 8:14-17)

When we encounter the Spirit, our spirits commune with God himself. That is why we are called "temples of the Holy Spirit." The Spirit dwelling within us makes us tabernacles of the living God. As Paul himself exclaims, "I have been crucified with Christ; and it is no longer I who live, but it is Christ who lives in me" (Gal 2:19-20). When we are led by the Spirit, his action within us flows into the other dimensions of our human makeup. This overflowing of the Spirit redounds to our souls, our bodies, and even our relationships with others. The transformation that God seeks to bring about within us begins in the spirit and spills into the other areas of our lives. The halo, that arc of light that surrounds the head of a saint, is an indication of the divinizing effect the Spirit has on the entire human person and, also, all of humanity.

The Social. As human beings we also form relationships with each other. This social dimension of our human makeup is built into the very fabric of our lives; it is hardwired into us. This all points to the fact that we are social creatures by nature. Without others in our lives, we would become stagnant and stale. Family and friends, the local community, churches we attend, the clubs and associations we belong to, the countries we live in, all these shape us into the persons whom we are. Another way of looking at it is through the lens of our Catholic faith. Since our Triune God—Father, Son, and Holy Spirit—is social by his very nature, it follows that we who are created in his image and likeness would also be social in nature. What is more, "God is love," we are told (1 Jn 4:16). Love involves a reciprocal exchange of giving and receiving, what C.S. Lewis refers to as "Gift Love" and "Need Love."[7] We are called to abide in God's love and to allow his love to shine in us and through us so it can touch others. This social dimension of our human makeup deepens our understanding of the Church as the Mystical Body of Christ. As the Apostle Paul reminds us: "For just as the body is one and has many members, and all the members of the body, though many, are one body, so it is with Christ. For in the one Spirit we were all baptized into one body—Jews or Greeks, slaves or free—and we were all made to drink of one Spirit" (1 Cor 12:12-13). When seen in this light, we belong not only to Christ but also to one another. Life in the Spirit transforms our relationships with others and incorporates them into a redeemed and divinized humanity with Christ at its head.

On Befriending Others

The above anthropological alignment takes on greater significance when we place it in the context

---

[7] C. S. Lewis, *The Four Loves*, 1-2.

of friendship with others. For one thing, it indicates that authentic friendships embrace every dimension of our human makeup: the physical, the intellectual/psychological, the spiritual, and the social. How this plays out will vary according to the nature of the friendship and the state of life to which the people in question belong. The physical dimension of friendship, for example, would mean different things for a married couple and two members of a religious order. Slight nuances would also apply to the other three dimensions of our human makeup. What is more, each of these dimensions can be viewed through the interpretative lenses of the various senses discussed in the previous chapter.

The physical dimension, for example, has not only a literal meaning, our bodily materiality, but also an allegorical, tropological (or moral), and anagogical sense. For the allegorical, the body points to the Mystical Body of Christ, the Church. For the tropological (or moral) sense, it points to the life of virtue and the gifts and fruits of the Spirit which help us in our fight against the flesh. For the anagogical sense, in turn, it points to the resurrection of the body and our glorified existence at the end of time. For the *intellectual/*

psychological dimension of our human makeup, the literal sense points to our intellect, will, and passions as we presently experience them. The allegorical sense, in turn, points to putting on the mind of Christ, conforming our wills to the will of God, and allowing our passions to be tamed by the grace of Christ's Spirit. For the *spiritual dimension* of our human makeup, the literal sense points to the deepest part of our hearts while the allegorical sense points to the Spirit of Christ who communes with our spirits and cries out, "Abba, Father" (Rom 8:15), and the tropological (or moral) sense points to the gifts and fruits of the Holy Spirit. Finally, for the *social dimension* of our human makeup, the literal sense pertains to the actual relationships we have in life. The allegorical sense, in turn, points to the friendship we have with Christ and with the members of his body, the Church, while the tropological (or moral sense) reflects the life we live in the Spirit and the growth in the Spirit we undergo by walking together the threefold way of purgation, illumination, and union. The anagogical sense of this dimension points to the communion of saints in heaven to which we hope we all will one day belong.

Befriending others involves encountering them in every dimension of their human makeup and viewing them through the eyes of the literal, allegorical, tropological (or moral), and anagogical senses. This anthropological alignment with the various literal and spiritual lenses as outlined above will enable us to view the person before us with a deeper understanding of who he or she is and a greater appreciation of the mystery we are engaging and with which we are seeking to bond.

Conclusion

We are social beings, and the desire for friendship is deeply embedded in our nature. This is so because we are created in the image and likeness of God, and he himself has desired our friendship from all eternity. "Love is self-diffusive," the saying goes.[8] The very reason why God created us is so he could enter into an intimate friendship with us. He seeks to befriend us and wants nothing more than for us to

---

[8] Pseudo-Dionysius, *On the Divine Names, 4.* See also Thomas Aquinas, *Summa theologiae*, I, q. 5, a. 4, obj. 2.

befriend him as well. Because of humanity's original fall from grace, however, we have desired not to follow the way of the Lord Jesus but to go it alone, even though it will lead us astray. God, however, refused to give up on us. To prove his love for us, he entered our world in the person of Jesus Christ and laid down his life for us to set us free from the slavery of sin and lead us in the way of Truth and Life.

Friendship with Christ leads us along the way of discipleship. When we follow him, we walk a path that leads to holiness and true freedom, one that enables us to follow the promptings of the Spirit, through whose grace we are empowered to live in a way that displays the Christian virtues and Spirit's grace-filled gifts and myriad fruits. Holiness and freedom also lead to the beatific vision, that face-to-face encounter with God for which we long and already sense deep within our hearts. Because of our friendship with Christ, his Spirit can dwell within our hearts, and we, in turn, are able to dwell within his glorified humanity.

When we befriend another person, we are befriending Christ himself. When doing so, we must take care to encounter and care for every dimension of that person: the physical, the intellectual/psychological, the spiritual, and the social. We must also view each of these dimensions in such a way that we can sense not only what these dimensions signify literally, but also what they tell us about Christ and his Church (the allegorical sense), the human person (the tropological or moral sense), and the world to come (the anagogical sense). This anthropological alignment of the various dimensions of our human makeup with these various interpretative lenses will enable us to see each human being as a unique icon of Christ, and someone who, like an icon itself, can lead us to a deeper encounter with the Word from which we came.

Reflection Questions

- How would you explain the difference between the "freedom of indifference" and the "freedom for excellence?" Are they complete opposites? Is there an element of truth in each of them? Which one, in your opinion, is the predominant understanding of freedom in today's world? Which offers a better understanding of true freedom?

- What is the relationship between freedom and holiness? What is their relationship to happiness? Who or what is the source of happiness? What must we do to attain it? What obstacles might get in the way? Is it possible to achieve the fullness of happiness in this life?

- What does the word "friendship" indicate to you? Do you think it is a much over used word today? What does it mean to befriend another person? Do you have any? How can the model of befriending presented in this chapter help you to encounter others on a deeper more authentic level?

- Is the desire for friendship hardwired into us? Is it part of our very nature to want to have deep, solid friendships to accompany us in life? What is the difference between an acquaintance and a friend? What is the difference between friendship of utility and pleasure? Between these and authentic friendships oriented toward the good?

- To what extent is friendship with Christ the key to building up the kingdom? To what extent is friendship with and in Christ the key to Christian discipleship. How would you describe your relationship with Christ? Do you have many friends in Christ? What role does the Spirit play in the building of such friendships?

Prayer to the Holy Spirit

Holy Spirit, Helper, I turn to you in time of need. Please, enlighten me with your gifts and fruits. Help me to befriend Jesus, my Lord and God, and all those I encounter throughout the day. Bestow on me the grace, the essence of the New Law. Help me to befriend others as the Lord has befriended me. In you I place my hope!

Chapter Five

Becoming a Divinized Person

God, the Father, seeks to befriend us. He sent his Son, Jesus Christ, to live among us and lay down his life for us. Jesus, in turn, has risen from the dead, ascended to heaven, and sent his Spirit to dwell within our hearts, so we can rest in Jesus' heart and through him be adopted sons and daughters of the Father. We are children of God because at Baptism we were immersed in his paschal Mystery and empowered by the Holy Spirit to share in Jesus' glorified humanity. Doing so means we hope one day to be fully divinized ourselves. Our friendships with Christ and others in Christ will pave the way for this to happen. The grace of the Spirit, the essence of the New Law, brings about this transformation in us, but in and through the relationships we share with Christ and others. Friendship with Christ, both individually and communally, takes place in and through the work of the Spirit in our lives. That work promises to transform us on every level of our human makeup: the physical, the intellectual/psychological, the spiritual, and the social.

This chapter will examine what our glorified humanity will look like. The goal of our existence, the very reason why God created us, is to become divinized persons who are members of Christ's Mystical Body. When seen in this light, our divinization (or deification, if you will) is but a small part of a larger creative action of God. Jesus, the New Adam, came to forge a New Creation out of the Old by breathing new life into a fallen world that had lost its way and was headed for the darkness of death and eternal isolation from God, others, and even our own selves. This new life extends not only to humanity but to the whole of creation. The Eucharist, the sacrament of this New Creation, is a foretaste of things that, at one and the same time, are already here yet still to come. This eschatological, already-but-not-yet, character of the sacrament, engages us on the level of faith and instills in us a hope that the reign of God, proclaimed by Christ and which has been planted in our hearts, will one day come to fruition in the lives of all believers and of all people of good will. This reign of God will be ruled by the Law of the Spirit and will govern Christ's kingdom for all eternity.

The Divinized Person

What do we mean by humanity's divinization? Just what does it entail? What does sharing in God's divinity signify? How are we to envision such a sharing? Where do we even begin to answer such questions? To understand this process of human transformation, we must understand the Christian doctrines of Creation, the Fall, the Incarnation, Redemption, and the sending of the Spirit at Pentecost. These doctrines are intimately related and shed light upon each other.

Creation. The Bible begins with two accounts of Creation. In the first (Gn 1-2:4) from the Priestly author, God creates the world and everything in it in six days. He does so not out of some primordial stuff or matter but out of nothing. What is more, he creates man and woman in his image and likeness on the sixth day, placing them at the summit of his creation. In the second account (Gn 2:5-24) from the Yahwist, he creates man at the outset of his creation and because of his original solitude that could be satisfied by no other creature, he fashions woman from a rib taken from his side to indicate that she is bone of his bone and flesh of his flesh and that they are equal partners in life. What is more, he makes them caretakers of the world and everything in it. There are a number of takeaways from these two accounts. Creation is good. God is the Creator. Human beings and everything in the world are creatures. Human beings were created in the image and likeness of God. They have been given the task to watch over creation, cultivate it, and make it fruitful. They themselves have also been given the task to be fruitful and multiply. Because they are created in God's image and likeness, they share in God's creative powers and procreators who bring new life into the world.

The Fall. The accounts of creation are followed by the story of the Fall (Gn 3:1-24). It is a symbolic story which captures something deeply rooted in humanity's collective consciousness, the sense that the present state of Creation is not as God had originally intended, that somewhere, somehow the world and everything in it had gone awry. The story of the Fall places the blame squarely on our first parents, Adam and Eve, who were placed in the Garden of Eden to enjoy lives in fellowship with their Creator. They had free rein to do as they pleased in this earthly paradise, and their only prohibition was not to eat the fruit of the Tree of the Knowledge of Good and Evil. While in Eden, they had access to the Tree of Life, the fruit of which all the blessings that life could bestow. They were tempted by the serpent, who told them the reason why God did not want them to eat fruit from that particular Tree was that doing so would make them like God with the power to decide what is good and what is evil, thus placing themselves (and not God) at the center of the moral universe. Because they were endowed with free will, their choice to follow their own will rather than God's had drastic effects on them and the whole of Creation. The result of this original fall from grace darkened Adam and Eve's minds, weakened their wills, made their passions unruly and out of sync, exposed them to death and bodily decay, and disrupted their social relations as evidence in the chapters immediately following their being cast out of the Garden. What is more, their fall from grace wounded human nature itself so that all of their progeny would suffer the same wounds for generations and generations to come. From then on, man would labor by the sweat of his brow and woman would suffer the pangs of childbirth. Humanity would also lose touch with the collective consciousness with which it had been blessed and would retain only a faint memory of it in their individual awareness.

The Incarnation. If humanity was credited for the topsy-turvy world in which it presently finds itself, God was responsible for healing it and initiating its gradual transformation into the New Creation. The means chosen for this to happen was for God to enter our world in the person of Jesus Christ to repair the damage done to Creation by the sin of our first parents from the inside out. There is some question as to whether God would have become man even if Adam and Eve had never sinned. Being God, he certainly could have, but such a question is moot since humanity's fall from grace did, in fact, occur and we are suffering the consequences of that tragic fall to this very day. There are others who question whether God had the power to unite his divinity with humanity in such a unique way (a hypostatic union) without blurring the boundaries between them. For such people, their idea of God is too small. God is all powerful and capable of entering the world he made. Just as man is "capable of God" (*capax Dei*), so God is "capable of man" (*capax hominis*). That is, he was powerful enough to make himself small enough to enter our world and by uniting his divinity to our humanity through the Virgin Mary's humble fiat, he paved the way for humanity's divinization and eventually the elevation of Creation to a higher order of existence. What is more, by entering our world by becoming one of us and choosing to redeem us by laying down his life for us through his death on the cross, he showed us the extent of God's love for us and his willingness to go to extreme lengths to save us from ourselves and the darkness we so often choose time and again over the light of the Gospel. Jesus entered the darkness of his mother's womb, that of the cave through which he was born, that of a fallen world, and ultimately into the darkness of hell itself, to bring us light and to reveal himself—"the way, and the truth, and the life" (Jn 14:6)—as the only way to the Father.

The Redemption. "God became man, so that man might become divine." As we have seen, these words of Athanasius of Alexandria remind us that the reason for the Incarnation was the redemption of the human race. God entered our world and became one of us in order to lay down his life for us, in order to heal us of our wounds, free us from the slavery of sin, and transform us, divinize us, so we could become his adopted sons and daughters. There are many ways in which theologians have tried to explain the mystery of redemption. During the patristic period, the ransom model held that Jesus' death on the cross was a ransom he paid to Satan that would pay the debt that humanity owed him due to Adam's sin. It was the way they interpreted the Gospel verse, "…the Son of Man came not to be served but to serve, and to give his life a ransom for many" (Mt 20:28). In the early twelfth century, Anselm of Canterbury (1033/34—1109) developed the satisfaction model of redemption in his *Cur Deus Homo?*, which took Satan out the picture and said that God became man and died on the cross so that the demands of God's justice would be satisfied by God's mercy. In that same century, Peter Abelard (c. 1079-1142) developed the moral model of redemption, which claimed that God became man and died on the cross for us to show us the depths of God's love for us. In the end, no single model can exhaust the full meaning of the mystery of Redemption. Each of the above models gives us a glimpse into the depths of this mystery, so perhaps they should be used in conjunction with one another to help us understand it. In the end, we don't need to know all the intricacies of why God chose to redeem us by becoming man and dying on the cross for us. We just need to believe that the means he chose, hidden from our minds as it is, has produced the fullness of redemption.

The Descent of the Holy Spirit. The cross led to the empty tomb. When Jesus rose from the dead, his humanity was transformed and glorified. He ascended to heaven to sit at the right hand of the Father, so he could send us his Spirit, who would continue his divinizing work through the body of believers he left behind. The Church as the body of Christ on earth continues Christ's divinizing action through her teachings and the administration of the sacraments, which are actions of Christ made present through visible signs and the grace of the Spirit. Three of these— Baptism, Confirmation, and the Eucharist—are sacraments of initiation, which immerse us into the redemptive action of Christ's paschal mystery (Baptism), strengthen us for the journey ahead (Confirmation), and give us food for the journey (Eucharist). Two of them—Marriage and Holy Orders—are sacraments of vocation which represent the love of Christ for his Church (Marriage) and are a visible sign of Christ's presence in our midst (Holy Orders). The final two—Reconciliation and the Anointing of the Sick—are sacraments of healing for the difficulties we face along the journey and as we approach death and prepare for our final journey beyond the bounds of this present life. Of these seven sacraments, the Eucharist is the most important. While the other six are actions of Christ, the Eucharist, the sacrament of sacraments, brings the actual person of Christ—body, blood, soul, and divinity—into our very midst, but hidden in the form of bread and wine. When we eat his body and drink his blood, Christ's divinization action continues within us by uniting our humanity to his glorified humanity and transforming us in such a way that we literally become members of his body and able to enter the presence of his Father. The Descent of the Holy Spirit on Pentecost represents the birth of Christ's body on earth.

The Spirit accompanies us throughout our lives through the sacraments and by dwelling within our hearts and dispensing among us his myriad gifts and fruits. To live in the Spirit is to follow the way of the Lord Jesus: to think like him, to act like him, to pray like him, to lay down our lives for others, as he did for us.

The New Adam

Jesus is often referred to as the "Second Adam." This title can be traced to the Apostle who said, "…as all die in Adam, so all will be made alive in Christ" (1 Cor 15:22) and again "…just as one man's trespass led to condemnation for all, so one man's act of righteousness leads to justification and life for all. For just as by the one man's disobedience the many were made sinners, so by the one man's obedience the many will be made righteous" (Rom 5:18-19). In the second century A.D., Irenaeus of Lyons (d c.180) extended this analogy by referring to Jesus as the "New

Adam" and to Mary as the "New Eve."[1] What exactly do we mean when we refer to Jesus by this title? Is it a mere metaphor, a poetic gesture meant to underscore the importance of Jesus' redemptive self-offering? Or is it something more? When we take a closer look at the term, it will become clear that the title ascribes to Jesus something more.

Key to understanding the meaning of this title is the two-fold meaning of "adam" in Hebrew to refer to not only to an individual (as in the person, Adam) but also to the collective whole (as in humanity or mankind). This two-fold meaning tells us something about human consciousness at the dawn of time. It referred to individuals, but it also pointed to their being connected to the larger whole. Before the Fall, we possessed not only an individual consciousness, but also a collective awareness. As a result, we had a strong sense of our common heritage and, made in the image and likeness of God, of being set apart from the rest of creation. Just as God was One but many, so, too, each of us had a strong sense of being

---

[1] Irenaeus of Lyons, *Against the Heresies,* 5.19.1; 20.2; 21.1

both individuals and members of a larger whole. One of the sad consequences of the Fall was that we lost this collective awareness and would expend much energy from then on trying to retrieve it. The building up of clans, tribes, kingdoms, nations, and empires gives witness to humanity's awareness of its social nature, as does the rise of culture and the quest for knowledge and wisdom. Still, after the Fall, humanity had lost the collective awareness of which today we see only vestiges in nature, as in how a colony of ants or a hive of bees behaves.

What does this have to do with calling Jesus the New Adam? If Jesus could restore everything humanity had lost on account of the Fall, then one of the things that we regained through him was that deep collective awareness. Jesus as the Second Adam refers to Jesus himself who rose from the dead and transformed his humanity—body, soul, and spirit—into a glorified humanity. That glorified humanity, in turn, had repercussions for physical, intellectual/psychological, spiritual, and social makeup. For example, his glorified risen body was not confined by the limits of time and space. It could walk through walls, be in two places at once, and even be present in the consecrated bread and wine of the Eucharistic table, while all the while he is sitting at the right hand of the Father in heaven. As far as his human soul is concerned, although it was never darkened by the effects of sin, because of the resurrection it was now elevated beyond its natural capacity. Its reason, will, interior senses of memory and imagination, and passions were all divinized and empowered to do things beyond their natural capacities. The same holds true for Jesus' human spirit which, because of the resurrection, now enjoyed an even deeper intimacy with the Holy Spirit and with the spirits of all humanity. Even Jesus' social relations were transformed as a result of the resurrection.

St. Paul's talk about our being members of Christ's body (1 Cor 12:12) is more than a mere metaphor. By the grace of the Spirit and the virtues of faith, hope, and charity, we literally form a part of the New Adam. The seeds of the New Creation have already by planted in our hearts and will grow to fruition both in this life and in the life to come. Our bodies will be glorified, our minds enlightened, our wills strengthened, our memories and imaginations deepened, our spirits completely open to the Holy Spirit, and our social relations rooted in the love of God. Best of all, we will have regained that collective awareness that we lost in the Fall. That collective consciousness is nothing other than the consciousness of Christ himself, whose Spirit wishes to take possession of our souls which, unlike Satanic possession, preserves our individual identities and brings them to their fullest expression by incorporating them into Jesus' own conscious awareness. The Apostle Paul reminds us of this gentle movement of the Spirit when he exhorts his readers thus:

> You were taught to put away your former way of life, your old self, corrupt and deluded by its lusts, and to be renewed in the spirit of your minds, and to clothe yourselves with the new self, created according to the likeness of God in true righteousness and holiness. (Eph 4:22-24)

By putting on Christ, the grace of the Spirit empowers us to become like him in all things. We think like him, act like him, walk with him, and even pray like him. Jesus said that he and the Father were one (Jn

10:30). Through the grace of the Spirit, we will become one in the Spirit and one with Christ, who will then lead us into the presence of the Father.

Conclusion

God created us to be his children. Even when we turned our backs on him, he never gave up on his dream for us. Rather than simply allowing us to go our own way, he sent his Son to us to show us the way back to him. Jesus of Nazareth, the Word of God and the Son of God, entered our world and became one of us, laid down his life for us to the point of dying for us on the cross, became nourishment for us by giving us his own body and blood to eat and drink, and became a source of hope for us by rising from the dead, returning to his heavenly Father, and sending us his Spirit to lead us to the place where Jesus has gone ahead and prepared for us.

God created and redeemed us to share in his life. He became one of us so that we might be one with him. Creatures though we are, he made us capable of enjoying a life of intimate friendship with him. He created us in such a way that, unlike all the rest of his creation, we could freely enter into relationship with him and, like Jesus himself, call God our Father. Because of Jesus, we, too, can become one with the Father. We, too, can see as he sees. We, too, can love as he loves. Jesus, the New Adam, has incorporated us into himself as members of his Mystical Body. He lives in us and acts through us. Each of us has a role to play in the building up of his kingdom. That is why each day we pray, "Thy kingdom come. Thy will be done, on earth as it is in heaven."

The irony of humanity's fall from grace is that Adam and Eve ate the forbidden fruit from the Tree of the Knowledge of Good and Evil because they wanted to be like God (Gn 3:5), when this was God's intention all along. They sought to become divine on their own merits when it was meant to be given them from the very outset. We are sons and daughters of our first parents, and we are free to make the same mistake they did so long, long ago. We are, however, also children of God, brothers and sisters of Our Lord, Jesus Christ, and sons and daughters of Our Father in heaven. We can listen to the temptations of the Evil One, or we can be guided by the promptings of the Spirit. One will lead us to our doom; the other will lead us to glory shared with the saints in heaven. The choice lies before us and is for us to make. Let us choose wisely. Let us listen to the voice of the dove and not to the cunning lies of the serpent.

Reflection Questions

- What is meant by the phrase "divinized person?" Does it erase the distinction between the Creator and his creatures? Does it apply to everyone? Can one be divinized against one's will? If divinization is our share in the intimacy of divine life, are there limits to this sharing? Can the process of divinization be reversed? If so, how?
- Why is it necessary to understand the doctrines of Creation, the Fall, Incarnation, Redemption, and Descent of the Holy Spirit to understand humanity's divinization? What do these doctrines tell us about humanity? What do they tell us about God? In what way is our divinization the result of these important Christian doctrines?

Chapter Five: Becoming a Divinized Person

- Why do we call Jesus the New Adam? What does he restore that the First Adam lost for humanity? To what extent are Jesus' disciples members of this New Adam? What is relationship between the New Adam and the doctrine of the Mystical Body of Christ? To what extent can we consider Mary the New Eve?
- Do you believe that Jesus, the New Adam, will restore the collective awareness humanity once shared but lost because of the Fall, while at the same time maintaining our own individual consciousness? What do you think such a collective awareness was like? Can you see any vestiges of it in the world around you?
- What is the irony of humanity's original fall from grace? How were our first parents deceived into disobeying God by thinking they could place themselves at the center of the moral universe? How did that fall from grace affect human nature? How did it affect their relationship with God?

Prayer to the Holy Spirit

Holy Spirit, My Love and Inspiration, help me to be in touch with your constant promptings. Fill me with your gifts and fruits. Help me to keep my eyes focused on the only thing that matters: God's will for me to become a divinized person destined to share in his intimate love. Help me, please help me. Without you, I can do nothing. Without you, I would be lost! With your help I will become a divinized person.

Conclusion

"God became human so that humanity might become divine." God's love is such that he wanted those he created in his image and likeness to share in his divinity. He made us capable of entering into an intimate friendship with him. He created us, in other words, to share in his inner life. The Holy Spirit, the bond between the Father and the Son, unites us to them through the outpouring of his grace. Without his help, we would be completely helpless to lead holy lives. We cannot even pray to God without his assistance.

The Spirit makes us holy not only as individuals but also as a collective whole. God "…desires everyone to be saved and to come to the knowledge of the truth" (1 Tm 2:4). We are all called to holiness. Our destiny lies not only in our individual sanctity but also in our corporate sanctity. We are saved primarily as a people and only secondarily as individuals. We are all members of Christ's Mystical Body. We each have a role to play within the body. The Apostle Paul says it best:

> Indeed, the body does not consist of one member but of many. If the foot would say, "Because I am not a hand, I do not belong to the body," that would not make it any less a part of the body. And if the ear would say, "Because I am not an eye, I do not belong to the body," that would not make it any less a part of the body. If the whole body were an eye, where would the hearing be? If the whole body were hearing, where would the sense of smell be? But as it is, God arranged the members in the body, each one of them, as he chose. If all were a single member, where would the body be? As it is, there are many members, yet one body. (1 Cor 12:14-20)

Jesus, the New Adam, lives in and through us. What we understand to be a person is too small a concept when it comes to him. Jesus, we can say, is "suprapersonal." He goes beyond our understanding of personhood not only because he is one of the Persons of the Blessed Trinity, but also because he can incorporate individual personal beings like us into himself. That is, he can preserve our individual identities, while also enabling us to share in what in him is both an individual and corporate identity. He accomplished this by becoming one of us, laying down his life for us, giving us his body and blood to eat and drink, and sending his Spirit to us to unite our humanity to his glorified humanity thus making us adopted sons and daughters of the Father. By communing with Christ in this way, we maintain our creaturely status while also becoming fully alive as the Spirit of Christ imparts to us a share in the intimate love shared by the Father and his Son, and the entire communion of saints in heaven. Such is God's vision for us. Let us work together with the Spirit as our guide to make this vision a reality.

www.ingramcontent.com/pod-product-compliance
Lightning Source LLC
Chambersburg PA
CBHW070853050426
42453CB00012B/2176